GW00726184

This compilation copyright © 1999 Lion Publishing

Published by
Lion Publishing plc
Sandy Lane West, Oxford, England
ISBN 0 7459 4039 0

First edition 1999
10 9 8 7 6 5 4 3 2 1 0

A catalogue record for this book is available
from the British Library

Typeset in 12/12.5 Venetian 301
Printed and bound in Singapore

Designer: Philippa Jenkins

secrets of
prayer

secrets of
prayer

Compiled by
Philip Law

Illustrated by
Grahame Baker Smith

LION
Giftlines

I don't say anything to God.
I just sit and look at him
and let him look at me.

ANONYMOUS
(19TH-CENTURY FRENCH PEASANT)

Whenever you pray, go into your room and shut the door and pray to your Father who is in secret; and your Father who sees in secret will reward you.

Jesus (Matthew 6:6)

When thou prayest, rather let
thy heart be without words
than thy words without heart.

JOHN BUNYAN

We are what we pray.

CARLO CARRETTO

Prayer is the effort to live in
the spirit of the whole.

SAMUEL TAYLOR COLERIDGE

If you pray truly, you
will feel within yourself
a great assurance: and
the angels will be your
companions.

EVAGRIUS OF PONTUS

Prayer is
the breathing of the soul.

JOHN OF KRONSTADT

Pray inwardly, even if you do not
enjoy it. It does good though you
feel nothing, even though you
think you are doing nothing.

JULIAN OF NORWICH

We need to find God
and he cannot be found
in noise and restlessness.
God is the friend of silence...
the more we receive in silent
prayer, the more we can give
in our active life.

MOTHER TERESA

Like a fish which at first
swims on the surface of
the water, and afterwards
plunges down and is
always going deeper, the
soul plunges, dives,
and loses itself in
the sweetness of
conversing
with God.

St John Vianney

The mind is not perfectly at
prayer until the one praying
does not think of himself
or know he is praying.

St Antony of Egypt

To pray
is to sit open-handed
before God.

PETER G. VAN BREEMEN

Our prayer has had a
beginning because we
have had a beginning.
But it will have no end.
It will accompany us
into eternity and will
be completed in our
contemplation of God.

CARLO CARRETTO

Pray as you can, and do
not try to pray as you can't.

JOHN CHAPMAN

When you pray,
you yourself must
be silent…
let the prayer speak.

TITO COLLIANDER

If your prayer is sincere, there will be every time you pray a new feeling containing an idea in it, an idea you did not know before, which will give you fresh courage.

FYODOR DOSTOEVSKY

To be silent, to suffer, to pray,
when there is no room for
outward action, is an
acceptable offering to God.

François Fénelon

Half an hour's listening
is essential except when
you are very busy. Then
a full hour is required.

St Francis of Sales

A good prayer, though often used, is still fresh and fair in the eyes and ears of heaven.

Thomas Fuller

When we
are linked
by the power
of prayer, we
hold each
other's hand,
as it were,
while we
walk along
a slippery
path.

ST GREGORY THE GREAT

At its highest peak prayer becomes contemplation. Here it is wordless. It is a merging of the human consciousness with the Divine.

BEDE GRIFFITHS

Do not turn to prayer hoping to enjoy spiritual delights; rather come to prayer totally content to receive nothing or to receive great blessing from God's hand, whichever should be your heavenly Father's will for you at that time.

Madame Jeanne Guyon

Prayer is
God being God in me being me.

TOM WRIGHT

God is a great
listener. Out of
his silent being,
he is with us
silently, he speaks
to us silently, he
asks us to learn
the response which
comes from the
deep part of our
being. He asks us
to learn from him
how to listen.

MICHAEL HOLLINGS

Certain thoughts are prayers.
There are moments when,
whatever be the attitude of the
body, the soul is on its knees.

VICTOR HUGO

The exercise of prayer, in those who habitually exert it, must be regarded by us doctors as the most adequate and normal of all pacifiers of the mind and calmers of the nerves.

WILLIAM JAMES

When you stand and pray, forgive anything you may have against anyone, so that your Father in heaven will forgive the wrongs you have done.

JESUS (MARK 11:25)

During the time of prayer the soul resembles a ship positioned in the middle of the sea. The mind is like the steersman in charge of the boat. The impulses convey the boat like the winds.

JOSEPH THE VISIONARY

Always long and pray that the will of God may be fully realized in your life. You will find that the man who does this walks in the land of peace and quietness.

THOMAS A KEMPIS

He who has learned to pray
has learned the greatest secret
of a holy and happy life.

WILLIAM LAW

To pray is to open oneself
to the possibility of sainthood,
to the possibility of becoming
set on fire by the Spirit.

KENNETH LEECH

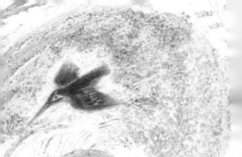

Prayer is like watching for the
Kingfisher. All you can do is
Be where he is likely to appear, and
Wait.

ANN LEWIN

Prayers are not always — in the crude, factual sense of the word — 'granted'. This is not because prayer is a weaker kind of causality, but because it is a stronger kind. When it 'works' at all it works unlimited by space and time.

C.S. Lewis

We do not even know how we
ought to pray, but through our
inarticulate groans the Spirit
himself is pleading for us,
and God who searches
our inmost being knows
what the Spirit means.

St Paul
(Romans 8:26)

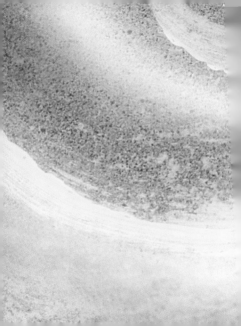

Prayer is an exercise of the spirit,
as thought is of the mind.

MARY F. SMITH

In every prayer an angel
waits for us, since every
prayer changes the one
who prays.

DOROTHÉE SOELLE

Before we
can hear the
Divine Voice we
must shut out all
other voices, so that
we may be able to listen,
to discern its faintest
whisper. The most precious
messages are those which
are whispered.

MARK RUTHERFORD

Is prayer your
steering wheel
or your spare tyre?

Corrie Ten Boom

Settle yourself in solitude
and you will come upon
Him in yourself.

St Teresa of Avila

Prayer means turning to Reality,
taking our part, however humble,
tentative and half-understood, in
the continual conversation, the
communion, of our spirits with
the Eternal Spirit… For prayer
is really our whole life toward God.

EVELYN UNDERHILL

When I began to pray with the heart, everything around me became transformed and I saw it in a new and delightful way. The trees, the grass, the earth, the air, the light and everything seemed to be saying to me that it exists to witness to God's love for us all and that it prays and sings of God's glory.

ANONYMOUS, THE WAY OF A PILGRIM

The best prayers
have often more
groans than words.

JOHN BUNYAN

The degree of our faith
is the degree of our prayer.
The strength of our hope
is the strength of our prayer.
The warmth of our charity
is the warmth of our prayer.

Carlo Carretto

He prayeth well who loveth wel
Both man and bird and beast;
He prayeth best who loveth bes
All things both great and small;
For the dear God who loveth us
He made and loveth all.

SAMUEL TAYLOR COLERIDGE

Strive never to pray
against anyone.

EVAGRIUS OF PONTUS

Prayer is a state of
continual gratitude.

JOHN OF KRONSTADT

f you want to pray better, you
must pray more. Prayer enlarges
the heart until it is capable of
containing God's gift of himself.

MOTHER TERESA

Prayer is the holy water
that by its flow makes the
plants of our good desires
grow green and flourish.

ST JOHN VIANNEY

Prayer takes the tangled ball of wool and gently untangles it, without snapping or cutting it.

Tom Wright

When you are praying, do not heap up empty phrases... for your Father knows what you need before you ask him.

Jesus (Matthew 6:7,8)

Acknowledgments

We would like to thank all those who have given us permission to include material in this book. Every effort has been made to trace and acknowledge copyright holders of all the quotations in this book. We apologize for any errors or omissions that may remain, and would ask those concerned to contact the publishers, who will ensure that full acknowledgment is made in the future.

Page 42: extract taken from 'Disclosure' in *Candles and Kingfishers* by Ann Lewin, published by The Methodist Publishing House.